DRUG & HOSPITAL
EMPLOYEES UNION RWDSU AFL-CIO

STUDENT TRAINEES
SUPPORT
SCHOOL
BOYCOTT

INTEGRATION
MEANS
BETTER
SCHOOLS
FOR ALL

DRUG & HOSPITAL
EMPLOYEES UNION

STUDENT TRAINEES
SUPPORT
SCHOOL
BOYCOTT

PERSPECTIVES ON THE
CIVIL RIGHTS MOVEMENT

by Heidi Deal

12 STORY LIBRARY

www.12StoryLibrary.com

12-Story Library is an imprint of Bookstaves and Press Room Editions

Produced for 12-Story Library by Red Line Editorial

Photographs ©: Harry Harris/AP Images, cover, 1; Everett Historical/Shutterstock Images, 4, 15; Gene Herrick/AP Images, 5, 10, 13; Hulton Archive/Archive Photos/Getty Images, 6; William Straeter/AP Images, 8; Bettmann/Getty Images, 9, 12; Horace Cort/AP Images, 11; Bill Allen/AP Images, 14; AP Images, 16, 18, 19, 22, 26, 27; Smith Collection/Gado/Archive Photos/Getty Images, 17; Bill Hudson/AP Images, 20; William J. Smith/AP Images, 23; Paul Cannon/AP Images, 24; Herman Hiller/New York World-Telegram and the Sun Newspaper Photograph Collection/Library of Congress, 25; Walt Zeboski/AP Images, 28; The San Francisco Examiner/AP Images, 29

Content Consultant: Françoise N. Hamlin, Associate Professor of Africana Studies and History, Brown University

Library of Congress Cataloging-in-Publication Data
Names: Deal, Heidi, 1979- author.
Title: Perspectives on the civil rights movement / by Heidi Deal.
Description: Mankato, MN : 12 Story Library, [2018] | Series: Perspectives on US history | Includes bibliographical references and index. | Audience: Grades 4-6.
Identifiers: LCCN 2016047357 (print) | LCCN 2016047929 (ebook) | ISBN 9781632353986 (hardcover : alk. paper) | ISBN 9781632354709 (pbk. : alk. paper) | ISBN 9781621435228 (hosted e-book)
Subjects: LCSH: African Americans--Civil rights--History--20th century--Juvenile literature. | Civil rights movements--United States--History--20th century--Juvenile literature. | Civil rights workers--United States--Biography--Juvenile literature | Racism--United States--History--20th century--Juvenile literature. | United States--Race relations--Juvenile literature.
Classification: LCC E185.61 .D395 2018 (print) | LCC E185.61 (ebook) | DDC 323.1196/073--dc23
LC record available at https://lccn.loc.gov/2016047357

Printed in the United States of America
022017

Access free, up-to-date content on this topic plus a full digital version of this book. Scan the QR code on page 31 or use your school's login at 12StoryLibrary.com.

Table of Contents

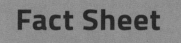

What led up to the civil rights movement?

After the US Civil War (1861–1865), Congress passed three amendments to the Constitution. One was supposed to give citizenship to all people born in the United States, regardless of race. All citizens were supposed to be treated equally under the law. That did not happen. Many states passed laws restricting the rights of black people. These became known as Jim Crow laws.

There were separate restaurants, bus services, and restrooms for black people. Politicians argued that segregation was legal. They claimed that as long as black people had their own facilities, the Constitution allowed such discrimination.

What happened during the civil rights movement?

Civil rights activists argued that the separate facilities were not equal. In 1954, the US Supreme Court ruled on *Brown v. Board of Education*.

Its verdict said that schools for black students did not provide the same educational opportunities that were available at the schools for white students. That ruling made segregation unconstitutional.

Brown v. Board of Education spurred activists to challenge segregation in other parts of everyday life. Organizations such as the Congress of Racial Equality (CORE) and the Student Nonviolent Coordinating Committee (SNCC) led protests and demonstrations. A minister named Martin Luther King Jr. led the Southern Christian Leadership Conference (SCLC) with nonviolent methods. Malcolm X and the Nation of Islam fought for racial pride.

What changed because of the civil rights movement?

Activists led demonstrations across the United States during the 1960s. Different organizations used different tactics. Segregationists tried to stop them and sometimes resorted to violence. But activists succeeded in pressuring the US government to pass the Civil Rights Act of 1964. This made it illegal to discriminate based on skin color or religion.

The NAACP Protects Black Rights

In 1909, a group of civil rights activists created the National Association for the Advancement of Colored People (NAACP). The NAACP was formed to stop violence against black people. It included both black and white men and women. The NAACP's membership grew quickly. It had offices all across the United States.

W. E. B. Du Bois (center) cofounded the NAACP.

90,000

Number of members the NAACP had after 10 years.

- The NAACP was created to stop violence against black people and make sure everyone had the same civil rights.
- The NAACP worked to put an end to lynching.
- The NAACP used lawsuits to fight for equal rights.

One big goal for the NAACP was to end lynching. Lynch mobs were groups of white people who attacked or killed black people. Some were organized by white supremacist groups such as the Ku Klux Klan (KKK).

Lynching was illegal in the early 1900s, but law enforcement at the time did little to stop it. The NAACP worked for many years to try to pass a new law about lynching. The law was first introduced in 1918. It was called the Dyer Bill. The bill would have guaranteed punishment for lynch mobs. It would have punished police officers for not arresting people who were seen lynching. The bill never passed. But attention from the NAACP helped reduce the number of lynchings after 1922.

The NAACP worked to hold people accountable to the law. It used lawsuits to fight for equal rights. Almost every court case during the civil rights movement was represented in some way by the NAACP.

THE KU KLUX KLAN

The Ku Klux Klan was started in the South after the Civil War. It shrank at the end of the 1800s, but it began to grow again in the 1910s. KKK members believed whites were superior. They used violence and intimidation against people of color and foreigners. KKK members wore white hoods and robes. They carried burning crosses. The KKK threatened and attacked civil rights supporters. They attacked and murdered black people.

The Little Rock Nine Desegregate Central High School

In 1954, the Supreme Court issued a ruling in the court case *Brown v. Board of Education*. It said there could not be separate schools for black students and white students. But in 1957, schools in Little Rock, Arkansas, were still segregated. The NAACP sued the Little Rock school board. As a result, the board agreed to let some black students attend Central High School.

Nine teenagers from black families were selected to attend the school. They were called the Little Rock Nine.

The Little Rock Nine tried to attend school on September 4, 1957. But they could not get in. The governor of Arkansas had called the National Guard. Guard members blocked the doors of the school.

The Little Rock Nine tried again on September 23. Many white residents were angry that that black students might go to school with their children. They gathered outside the school. They shouted and fought. The violence got so bad that the black students had to leave.

President Dwight D. Eisenhower sent the US Army to make sure that the

Daisy Bates (left) was the president of the NAACP's Arkansas chapter.

Elizabeth Eckford ignores mobs on her way to school.

1,200
Number of US Army soldiers deployed to ensure the safety of the Little Rock Nine.

- Nine black students called the Little Rock Nine were selected to integrate Central High School.
- The governor of Arkansas ordered the National Guard to keep the black students out.
- When the Little Rock Nine tried to go to school, mobs of white people screamed and threw things at them.
- The Little Rock Nine were finally able to attend school after President Eisenhower sent the US Army to keep the peace.

black students could safely enter the school. The Little Rock Nine finally attended a full day of school on September 25. At the end of the school year, the governor closed all Little Rock public schools to prevent integration.

ELIZABETH ECKFORD

The Little Rock Nine planned to enter the school as a group for safety. They chose a site to meet at in advance. But on September 4, NAACP leaders changed the meeting place at the last minute. Elizabeth Eckford did not know this. She arrived at the school alone. Mobs of white people screamed and threw things at her. Photographers took pictures. The pictures became famous all around the world.

The MIA Leads the Montgomery Bus Boycott

In the 1950s, bus seating was segregated in Montgomery, Alabama. Black people had to sit in the back. They often had to give up their seats to white passengers. Bus drivers often treated them poorly, too.

Activist Jo Ann Robinson and the Women's Political Council (WPC) wanted this unfair treatment to end. They asked city officials to change the racist practices. But the officials ignored them.

In 1955, a bus driver told activist Rosa Parks to give her seat to a white man. Parks refused. She was arrested. In response, the WPC and activist leader E. D. Nixon planned a one-day bus boycott. They protested against segregated bus seating. More than 90 percent of the black community participated in the boycott. They did not take buses. Instead, they walked or carpooled.

Later that day, boycott leaders met with a group of ministers and local activists. They agreed to keep the bus boycott going. The leaders at the meeting became the Montgomery Improvement Association (MIA). They asked Martin Luther King Jr. to be president of the group. This was

Rosa Parks's arrest provided the opportunity to protest that activists were looking for.

Empty buses during the boycott caused the city to lose money.

King's first major role in the civil rights movement.

The MIA organized and supported the yearlong bus boycott. It was a nonviolent protest. MIA members asked for three things. First, they wanted to be treated with respect by white bus drivers. Second, they wanted to end segregated seating. Third, they wanted black people to be hired as bus drivers for routes in black neighborhoods.

Boycotters faced many challenges and dangers. But churches and volunteers helped keep the boycott going. They collected donations and provided transportation. Their patience paid off. In November 1956, the Supreme Court ruled that segregated bus seating was illegal. Montgomery buses were desegregated one month later.

381

Number of days the Montgomery bus boycott lasted.

- The original boycott was scheduled for one day.
- After the first day, the MIA supported the boycott and kept it going.
- Boycotters walked, carpooled, or took church-provided vehicles.
- The boycott ended when buses were desegregated in December 1956.

THINK ABOUT IT

Can you think of an issue or problem that you could protest with a boycott?

4

The WCC Fights to Keep Segregation

Many white people were unhappy with the Supreme Court's decision to desegregate schools. They believed black people were inferior. They did not think black people should have the same rights as whites. The White Citizens' Council (WCC) was formed to preserve segregation without resorting to physical violence.

The WCC's first chapter was formed in Mississippi in 1954. New WCC chapters sprang up quickly across the South. The WCC made newsletters, TV shows, and radio programs. They told how segregation helped whites. WCC members threatened black people who fought for equal treatment. Some members were doctors, bankers, politicians,

People wave Confederate flags in support of segregation at this WCC meeting in New Orleans, Louisiana.

$2

Cost of an annual subscription to the *Citizens' Council,* the WCC's monthly white supremacist newspaper.

- The WCC wanted to prevent integration in states in the South.
- WCC members included judges, sheriffs, teachers, and governors.
- Weekly TV and radio programs supported segregation.
- WCC members worked to end the Montgomery bus boycott by using intimidation.

Montgomery mayor W. A. Gayle joined the WCC when the bus boycott started.

or business owners. They used their positions in society to support segregation. Some took away the homes or jobs of people who spoke in favor of integration.

The Montgomery bus boycott caused white business owners to lose money. The WCC wanted to end the boycott as quickly as possible. Some WCC members were on the police force. They arrested boycott organizers. Other WCC members forced taxi drivers to charge at least 45 cents per ride. That made it hard for low-income families to use taxis instead of buses.

Many white political and community leaders were part of the WCC. This made many white citizens see participation in the WCC as respectable. They believed that preventing desegregation was legal and just.

5

The SCLC Works to End Segregation

After the success of the Montgomery bus boycott, civil rights leaders wanted to expand their efforts. In February 1957, Martin Luther King Jr. invited black ministers to meet in Atlanta, Georgia. He wanted to talk about ending segregation. King and the church leaders formed the Southern Christian Leadership Conference (SCLC).

With Martin Luther King Jr. leading, the SCLC became one of the most active groups of the civil rights movement. The SCLC did not spend time recruiting individual members. Instead, it focused on partnering with other organizations. It worked with them to achieve common goals. The SCLC was open to people of all races and religions. Members used nonviolent action, such as sit-ins, marches, and boycotts. They helped organize major events to get the public's attention. They argued that segregation was morally wrong.

In 1963, the SCLC partnered with organizations such as the Negro American Labor Council (NALC) and the Student Nonviolent Coordinating Committee (SNCC). They planned to protest in Washington, DC. On August 28, thousands of activists took part in the March on Washington. During the march,

A group organized by the SCLC protests the arrests of civil rights demonstrators.

200,000
Estimated number of people who took part in the March on Washington.

- The SCLC practiced nonviolent action such as sit-ins and marches.
- Rather than recruit individual members, the SCLC partnered with many other civil rights organizations.
- The SCLC helped organize the 1963 March on Washington.

Marchers gathered on the National Mall during the March on Washington.

Martin Luther King Jr. gave his famous "I Have a Dream" speech. The speech focused on the idea of the American Dream. King explained how this idea had not been realized for all citizens.

The March on Washington got the attention of the US government. The Civil Rights Act was passed just one year later.

MARTIN LUTHER KING JR.

Martin Luther King Jr. was a Baptist preacher from Atlanta. He led many great events and gave many influential speeches during the civil rights movement. He wrote his famous "Letter from Birmingham Jail" in April 1963. King had been jailed for protesting. He wrote the letter on scraps of newspaper while he was in solitary confinement. The letter asked white church leaders in Birmingham to change their view on segregation. King was assassinated by a white supremacist in April 1968 in Memphis, Tennessee.

6

SNCC Commits to Direct Action to Gain Rights

On February 1, 1960, four black students sat at a lunch counter in Greensboro, North Carolina. Staff would not wait on them. The students refused to leave until they were served. By the end of the week, more students had joined them.

Students participate in a sit-down strike at a supermarket lunch counter in Houston, Texas.

Sit-in protests spread across the South at libraries, hotels, and other segregated places.

Civil rights leader Ella Baker wanted to help students organize their protests. She set up a meeting at Shaw University in North Carolina in April 1960. Baker helped student leaders form SNCC.

At first, SNCC members agreed to use nonviolence. They protested by marching, sitting, or singing. They stayed peaceful even when white citizens or police attacked them. Members also spent many hours working to register black voters.

In the mid-1960s, SNCC began to change. Leaders and members questioned its nonviolent tactics. Some wanted to exclude white

4
Number of students who first participated at the lunch counter sit-in in Greensboro, North Carolina.

- The peaceful lunch counter sit-ins led to the creation of SNCC.
- In the early 1960s, SNCC members took part in nonviolent protests and did not fight back when attacked.
- SNCC members worked to register black voters.
- Later, SNCC became more militant.

people from SNCC to promote black leadership. The changes strained SNCC's relationship with other civil rights organizations. By the end of the 1960s, SNCC had dissolved.

ELLA BAKER

Ella Josephine Baker was a civil rights activist. She worked with many organizations, including the NAACP and SCLC. Baker taught others how to organize and protest. She helped them draw attention to the civil rights movement. Her nickname was Fundi. It is a Swahili word that means "person who teaches a craft to the next generation."

Felt

YOUTH LEADERSHIP MEETING
SHAW UNIVERSITY
RALEIGH, N.C. – APRIL 15-17, 1960

WHY THIS MEETING?

Recent lunchcounter Sit-ins and other nonviolent protests by students of the South are tremendously significant developments in the drive for Freedom and Human Dignity in America.

The courageous, dedicated and thoughtful leadership manifested by hundreds of Negro students on college campuses, in large cities and small towns, and the overwhelming support by thousands of others, present new challenges for the future. This great potential for social change now calls for evaluation in terms of where do we go from here. The Easter week-end conference is convened to help find the answers. Together, we can chart new goals and achieve a more unified sense of direction for training and action in Nonviolent Resistance.

WHO WILL ATTEND?

Representation is invited from all areas of recent protest. However, to be effective, a leadership conference should not be too large. For this reason, each community is being asked to send a specified number of youth leaders. Adult Freedom Fighters will be present for counsel and guidance, but the meeting will be youth centered.

SCHEDULE:

The opening session will be Friday, April 15 at 7:30 o'clock. Saturday will be devoted to workshops, buzz-sessions and committee work. There will be a public meeting Saturday night, and the conference will close at lunchtime Sunday.

EXPENSES:

We believe that your community will want to help share your travel expenses; and the Southern Christian Leadership Conference hopes that housing and meals will be underwritten. The total cost for six (6) meals and housing for two (2) nights will be $6.30 per person.

FOR FURTHER INFORMATION, Contact the Southern Christian Leadership Conference, 208 Auburn Avenue, N. E., Atlanta, Ga..

Dr. Martin L. King, Jr.
President

Ella J. Baker
Executive Dire

A flyer advertising the student leadership meeting at Shaw University

Freedom Riders Test Desegregation of Interstate Buses

By 1960, the Supreme Court had ruled segregation illegal on interstate buses and bus stations. But many states in the South did not follow the Supreme Court's ruling. The Congress of Racial Equality (CORE) wanted to test the law's effects. They wanted the president to take action.

CORE planned Freedom Rides. In May 1961, Freedom Riders planned to travel from Washington, DC, to New Orleans on two buses. Many of them were students and young adults. They were committed to nonviolence. But they were often attacked or beaten.

On May 14, 1961, a white mob attacked one bus in Anniston, Alabama. The mob slashed tires and firebombed the bus. They attacked the Freedom Riders, too. The other bus continued to Birmingham,

Freedom Riders use a white waiting room in the Birmingham, Alabama, bus station.

The mob threw a firebomb through the bus's window during the Anniston attack.

Alabama. There, that bus and its riders were also attacked.

Journalists wrote about the Riders. Photographers took pictures. They showed mob members beating the Riders with baseball bats and pipes. These stories and pictures inspired more people to become Freedom Riders. They got the attention of the US government. On May 29, 1961, US Attorney General Robert Kennedy signed an order. It would enforce stricter guidelines against segregation on interstate buses. But the Freedom Rides continued until the order took effect in the fall.

15

Number of minutes the Birmingham police allowed the KKK to attack Freedom Riders before stopping the violence.

- Freedom Rides tested desegregation on buses in the South.
- The Riders remained peaceful even when attacked.
- Media coverage of violence against Freedom Riders forced the government to enforce bus desegregation.

THINK ABOUT IT

How do you think nonviolent protests helped black people influence the public's opinion during the civil rights movement?

Birmingham Police Enforce Segregation

Across the United States, many police organizations supported segregation. They kept enforcing it, even after the US Supreme Court ruled it unconstitutional. Birmingham police officers were no different. They did not stop white supremacists from attacking protesters. Officers were also known for brutality when arresting protesters. Some officers were members of the WCC and the KKK.

On May 2, 1963, SCLC organized a protest. It was called the Children's Crusade. Hundreds of children marched in the streets to protest segregation. Birmingham police arrested hundreds of the child

Police dogs attack a 17-year-old civil rights activist.

THINK ABOUT IT

Should children be allowed to participate in protests? Why or why not?

6

Age of the youngest protesters in the Children's Crusade.

- Police officers across the nation and in Birmingham protected white rights and enforced segregation.
- Police officers used high-powered fire hoses and police dogs on child protesters.
- Pictures of the police brutality forced city leaders to meet with civil rights activists.

protesters. More children came the next day. The commissioner of public safety ordered the police to turn the protesters away. Officers were told to use high-powered fire hoses, electric cattle prods, police dogs, and clubs.

Journalists took pictures of the children being arrested. They showed the officers' brutality. People across the nation were shocked to see images of children being attacked by police dogs. Businesses in the area suffered. US Attorney General Kennedy forced city leaders to meet with activists. On May 10, signs segregating restrooms and drinking fountains were removed in Birmingham. The disturbances moved President John F. Kennedy to give his first significant speech on civil rights in June.

BULL CONNOR

Eugene "Bull" Connor was a political leader in Birmingham for 22 years. As commissioner of public safety, he ordered the police to use force during the Children's Crusade. He used his control of the police to keep the city segregated. Connor was proud of his white supremacist policies. He was supported by white citizens of Birmingham. He was friendly with local KKK members, too.

21

Freedom Summer Activists Speak Out for Voting Rights

In the 1960s, many black people in Mississippi were denied the right to vote. Their applications to vote were often rejected. Others were forced to take tests or pay fees before they could vote. Some even faced threats on their lives.

Civil rights activists in Mississippi wanted people all around the country to know about these unfair practices. So they started the Freedom Summer campaign in 1964. The activists helped more people register to vote. They also called for a federal law to protect voting rights.

However, almost all lawmakers in Mississippi's Democratic Party were white. Most supported segregation laws. The Mississippi Democratic

Activists protest exclusion from the Democratic National Convention.

Activist Fannie Lou Hamer (center) was one of the MFDP's founders.

Party did not allow black people to participate in its meetings.

So civil rights activists formed their own political party. They called it the Mississippi Freedom Democratic Party (MFDP). The MFDP held its own meetings. It selected its own delegates for the 1964 Democratic National Convention (DNC). The delegates spoke out against the tactics used to keep black people in Mississippi from voting. They helped the voting rights campaign gain the attention of people all over the United States. In the end, the DNC chose the all-white delegates. However, the MFDP showed that a local movement could affect national politics. In 1965, the Voting Rights Act ended fees and literacy tests for black voters.

60,000
Number of black voters registered in Mississippi during Freedom Summer.

- Many black people in Mississippi were denied the right to vote.
- The Freedom Summer campaign was started by civil rights activists in Mississippi.
- The activists formed the Mississippi Freedom Democratic Party (MFDP).
- The MFDP's delegates helped bring national attention to the way black citizens were denied the right to vote.

The Nation of Islam Promotes Racial Pride

The Nation of Islam (NOI) was a religious group. Wallace D. Fard created it in 1930. During the civil rights movement, its leader was Elijah Muhammad. The NOI focused on teaching a version of Islam. It believed black people should start their own communities away from whites. It encouraged blacks to own their own businesses and work with other black-owned companies.

Elijah Muhammad (center) taught that black people were specially chosen by God.

INTERNATIONAL AMPHITHEATRE

50

Number of Nation of Islam Temples established by 1959.

- The NOI was founded in 1930 and teaches a version of Islam.
- NOI members believed black people should establish their own society separate from white people.
- NOI members did not think nonviolent tactics were effective enough.
- New members replaced their last name with an X to remove any link to slavery.

MALCOLM X

Malcolm X became a minister for the NOI in 1954. He spoke often of freedom and justice. He disagreed with nonviolent methods used by other organizations during the civil rights movement. He was particularly critical of Martin Luther King Jr. and the SCLC. Malcolm X later split with the NOI. He was assassinated by NOI members in 1965.

The NOI was not interested in integration. Leaders of the NOI said that white people were naturally bad. They believed that God wanted black people to rise above whites.

The Autobiography of Malcolm X tells the life story of this dynamic speaker and leader.

NOI members sometimes criticized other civil rights groups for working with white people. They also questioned whether nonviolent methods were effective. Some believed these methods were too slow to produce any real results. Instead, NOI members believed in using self-defense. This was especially true as segregationists became more brutal.

During slavery, black people were often given last names by slaveholders. When people joined the NOI, many replaced their last name with an *X*. The *X* removed their enslaved name. Later, the leaders of NOI gave members new last names that matched their personalities.

Lyndon B. Johnson Aims to Improve Equality

On November 22, 1963, John F. Kennedy was assassinated. Lyndon B. Johnson became the 36th US president. Johnson worked to improve equality in society. He signed the Civil Rights Act of 1964. Martin Luther King Jr. stood behind him as he did so. The act outlawed discrimination in public places. It also protected all citizens' right to vote.

Johnson signed the Voting Rights Act of 1965. This act ended poll taxes and literacy tests for black people. He chose Thurgood Marshall as the first black Supreme Court justice. Johnson also signed the Civil Rights Act of 1968, which outlawed housing discrimination.

Civil rights activists pressured Johnson to offer government services and help to minorities and the poor. His administration created

Lyndon B. Johnson discusses civil rights with NAACP leader Roy Wilkins.

Thurgood Marshall speaks with Elizabeth Eckford.

many education programs, including Head Start. This program helped disadvantaged preschoolers. Johnson started other programs, too. Some created paying jobs for the poor. Others provided medical care for the elderly.

Despite these government responses, racial relations were bad. People in black communities still faced discrimination, poverty, and unfair treatment. But Johnson's willingness to listen to civil rights activists helped pave the way for many improvements in American communities.

61

Percentage of votes Johnson received in the 1964 presidential election.

- Johnson became president in 1963 after John F. Kennedy was assassinated.

- Johnson signed the Civil Rights Act of 1964, the Voting Rights Act of 1965, and the Civil Rights Act of 1968.

- Thurgood Marshall became the first black US Supreme Court justice in 1967.

- Johnson started government programs such as Head Start to address poverty.

The Black Panther Party for Self-Defense Forms

The Black Panther Party was formed in 1966. It was originally called the Black Panther Party for Self-Defense. Huey P. Newton and Bobby Seale formed it to help black people protect one another from police harassment and brutality. Black Panthers were frustrated with the nonviolent tactics of other civil rights activists. Group members patrolled black neighborhoods with weapons to protect residents from harm.

The Black Panther movement began in Oakland, California. New Black Panther offices opened all across the country. By the end of the 1960s, the Black Panthers had more than 40 offices and 2,000 members. Unlike the NOI, the Black Panthers had no religious ties. They worked with both black and white groups. They believed in Black Power. This was the idea that black people should work to have economic and political influence.

Armed Black Panthers protest in the capitol building in Sacramento, California.

35
Number of survival programs started by the Black Panthers to assist the black community.

- The Black Panthers were created as a way for black people to protect one another from police brutality.
- Black Panthers wanted to fight back against economic inequality.
- Black Panthers were frustrated with nonviolent tactics.

Bobby Seale (left) and Huey P. Newton in Oakland, California

The Black Panthers were particularly concerned about economic inequality. They started survival programs to help black communities. They offered legal help and transportation. They even provided free shoes and free breakfast for kids.

The Black Panthers also opposed gun control. They believed they needed guns to protect themselves from police brutality. In 1967, some politicians supported a law limiting who could carry firearms. The Black Panthers saw this law as a way for the government to keep them from being able to defend themselves. They believed the law violated the 2nd Amendment of the US Constitution, which gives all citizens the right to bear arms. To protest, they marched and carried weapons. They marched into the capitol building in Sacramento, California. The march helped the Black Panther movement gain nationwide recognition.

Glossary

activist
A person who uses action to change rules or laws.

assassinated
Killed unexpectedly for political or religious reasons.

boycott
To refuse to buy something or do business with someone until change is made.

civil rights
The rights of all citizens to be treated equally.

delegate
A person who is chosen to vote or act as a representative for others.

desegregate
To stop dividing people into separate groups or locations based on race.

federal
Relating to the central government that unites and controls all 50 states in the United States.

minorities
People from a different ethnic group or religion than the larger group of people in the place where they live.

mob
A large, angry crowd.

protest
An event at which people gather to show they do not support something they believe is wrong or unfair.

segregated
When people are divided into separate groups or locations based on race.

For More Information

Books

Freedman, Russell. *Because They Marched: The People's Campaign for Voting Rights That Changed America*. New York: Holiday House, 2014.

Levinson, Cynthia. *We've Got a Job: The 1963 Birmingham Children's March*. Atlanta, GA: Peachtree Publishers, 2011.

Rubin, Susan Goldman. *Freedom Summer: The 1964 Struggle for Civil Rights in Mississippi*. New York: Holiday House, 2014.

Sepahban, Lois. *12 Incredible Facts about the Montgomery Bus Boycott*. North Mankato, MN: 12-Story Library, 2016.

Visit 12StoryLibrary.com

Scan the code or use your school's login at **12StoryLibrary.com** for recent updates about this topic and a full digital version of this book. Enjoy free access to:

- Digital ebook
- Breaking news updates
- Live content feeds
- Videos, interactive maps, and graphics
- Additional web resources

Note to educators: Visit 12StoryLibrary.com/register to sign up for free premium website access. Enjoy live content plus a full digital version of every 12-Story Library book you own for every student at your school.

Index

About the Author

Heidi Deal lives in Southern California with her family. She enjoys taking her two kids on adventures to explore science, nature, and history and creating stories to share with them.